Paul at Damascus

Story by Penny Frank
Illustrated by Eric Ford

Guideposts
50

CARMEL • NEW YORK 10512

The Bible tells us how God sent his Son Jesus to show us what God is like and how we can belong to God's kingdom.

When Jesus had gone back to be with God, the disciples were given the work of telling the whole world about Jesus and God's kingdom. Paul, an important man in Jerusalem, was one of those who tried to stop them.

You can find this story in your own Bible, in the book of Acts, chapter 9.

Copyright © 1986 Lion Publishing

Published by
Lion Publishing plc
Icknield Way, Tring, Herts, England
Lion Publishing Corporation
1705 Hubbard Avenue, Batavia,
Illinois 60510, USA
Albatross Books Pty Ltd
PO Box 320, Sutherland, NSW 2232, Australia

First edition 1986
Reprinted 1987

Printed and bound in Hong Kong by Mandarin Offset Marketing (HK) Ltd
This Guideposts edition is published by special arrangement with Lion Publishing

British Library Cataloguing in Publication Data

Frank, Penny
  Paul at Damascus. – (The Lion Story Bible; v.50)
  1. Paul, *the Apostle, Saint* – Juvenile literature 2. Bible stories, English – N.T. Acts
  I. Title   II. Ford, Eric, *1931* –
  226'.60924   BS2506.5

Library of Congress Cataloging-in-Publication Data

Frank, Penny.
  Paul at Damascus.
  (The Lion Story Bible; 50)
  1. Paul, the Apostle, Saint—Juvenile literature. 2. Christian saints— literature. 2. Christian saints— Turkey—Tarsus—Biography— Juvenile literature. 3. Tarsus (Turkey)— Biography—Juvenile literature.
  [1. Paul, the Apostle, Saint. 2. Bible stories—N.T.] I. Ford, Eric, ill. II. Title III. Series: Frank, Penny. Lion Story Bible; 50.
  BS2506.5.F72 1986   226'.609505
  85-23855

Paul was a leader in Jerusalem.
Everyone knew him. He was very clever
and he served God. Many people came
to him for advice, because he knew so
much about God's Law.

Paul had heard a lot about the disciples of Jesus Christ. They had been very afraid when Jesus had been killed. They just hid away together in a little room.

But now they had changed, and they seemed to be everywhere. They worshipped in the temple, they preached on the street corners.

There was even news of people being healed by the disciples in the name of Jesus.

Paul did not believe that Jesus really was God's Son. He did not know that God had given the disciples the special help of his Holy Spirit. Paul thought they were just making trouble.

So he set out with his friends to stop them.

Paul went from house to house. When he found people who talked about Jesus and the kingdom of God, he dragged them out of their homes and took them off to prison. Some of them died.

The priests and leaders in Jerusalem thought he was doing a splendid job.

One day, Paul set out from Jerusalem to the city of D'amascus. He had heard that some of Jesus' followers were there.

But, as he was going along the road, a blinding light suddenly shone down on him. It made his eyes hurt so much that he could not see.

Then a voice called to him. He could hear it clearly.

'Paul!' shouted the voice. 'Paul!'

'Who are you?' asked Paul. 'I can't see anything with this blazing light. Tell me who you are.'

'My name is Jesus,' was the answer. 'I am the one you are fighting against. You are wrong, Paul. I am alive. Get up now, and go into Damascus. Wait there until you are told what to do.'

Paul was amazed. He could not argue with the voice. He could not see the bright light any more. Everything was dark. Paul, the strong leader, was blind and helpless.

The friends who were with Paul had heard the voice but they could not see anyone there.

They helped Paul get up from the ground. They led him by the hand, as he stumbled into Damascus.

No one was afraid of Paul when he arrived in Damascus. For three days he just sat in the house.

He could not see anything. He did not want to eat or drink.

All he could think about was what had happened on the way.

Paul did not know that God was sending
someone to help him.

The man's name was Ananias and he
belonged to God's kingdom. He had
heard about Paul and the terrible things
he had done. He knew why Paul had
come to Damascus.

God spoke to Ananias.

'Ananias,' he said. 'I have something I want you to do for me today.'

'I want you to visit a man called Paul, who is staying in Damascus,' God said.

'But I can't do that,' gasped Ananias. 'He is our worst enemy. He has come to Damascus to take your people back to prison in Jerusalem.'

God told Ananias what had happened to Paul on his way to Damascus.

'I have told him that you are going to come and make him see again,' God said.

Poor Ananias! He was so afraid.

'Don't worry,' God said to Ananias.
'I have chosen Paul for very special
work. I am going to change him, just as
I have changed you. He will tell many
nations about me, although that will not
be an easy job for him.'

So Ananias made his way through the streets of Damascus to the house where Paul was staying. Ananias trusted in God and he knew God had given him the special power that Jesus had.

But he did wonder what was going to happen next.

Ananias knocked at the door and went into the house where Paul was. He put his hands on Paul's shoulders.

'Brother Paul,' he said, 'God has sent me so that you can see again and receive the gift of his Holy Spirit.'

At once Paul could see again. He knew now that Jesus was the Son of God. Everything Jesus' followers said about him was true. Paul no longer wanted to punish them. Instead he wanted to help them tell the whole world the good news about Jesus.

The people in Damascus could not believe their eyes when they saw the way Paul had changed.

'We thought Paul had come to take us off to prison,' they said. 'But now he can't stop talking about Jesus.'

Paul's old friends could not think what had come over him.

'How can Paul be a follower of Jesus,' they said. 'We can't believe it.'

But it was true. God had chosen Paul, the man who had done so much harm, to take the good news of Jesus to people of many nations.

The Story Bible Series from Guideposts is made up of 50 individual stories for young readers, building up an understanding of the Bible as one story—God's story—a story for all time and all people.

The Old Testament story books tell the story of a great nation—God's chosen people, the Israelites—and God's love and care for them through good times and bad. The stories are about people who knew and trusted God. From this nation came one special person, Jesus Christ, sent by God to save all people everywhere.

The New Testament story books cover the life and teaching of God's Son, Jesus. The stories are about the people he met, what he did and what he said. Almost all we know about the life of Jesus is recorded in the four Gospels—Matthew, Mark, Luke and John. The word gospel means 'good news.'

The last four stories in this section are about the first Christians, who started to tell others the 'good news,' as Jesus had commanded them—a story which continues today all over the world.

The story of how God chose Paul to tell people about Jesus comes in the New Testament book of Acts, chapter 9, and is recounted again in Acts, chapters 22 and 26.

Paul had one of the most dramatic conversion (or turnaround) stories of all time. But God wants each of us to 'turnaround' too: to stop going our own way and begin to go his way. By his death for us and his coming to life again, Jesus has made it possible for us to start again, to have a new life as his followers.